BY BRIAN BESTALL

Why Should I Learn Drum Rudiments?

Discover the beauty of drum rudiments and the numerous combinations that can be applied to the drum kit.

1 EDITION

Contents
Lessons 1–45

To my wife Rebecca, without whose help, support, encouragement and belief this book would never have been published.
To my children Lee, Nicky and Claire who have endured many hours of strange rhythms over the years.
Finally, to all my students past and present who have provided the inspiration for this book.

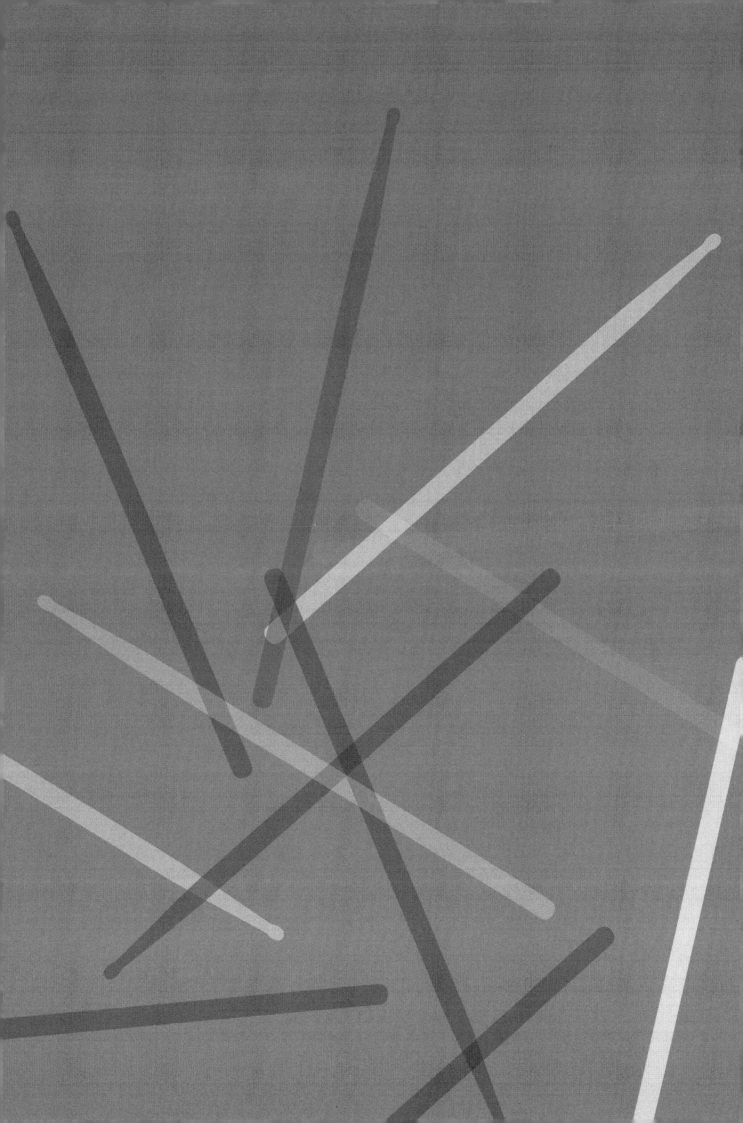

Introduction
By Brian Bestall

I've been teaching drums for over 25 years and the most frequently asked question is **"Why should I learn drum rudiments?"** My answer is simple: These rudiments are our vocabulary, a nod to our heritage and a way to help you to develop the four basic strokes; full stroke, down stroke, tap stroke and up stroke, and ultimately gain better stick control. By becoming proficient with these rudiments, you will become a more competent and confident player. You will learn to integrate them into your everyday playing, creating exciting grooves and fills.

The next question is **"How do I apply these rudiments to my kit?"** That's where we start our journey into the beautiful world of rudiments and the reason I was inspired to write this book.

How to use this book

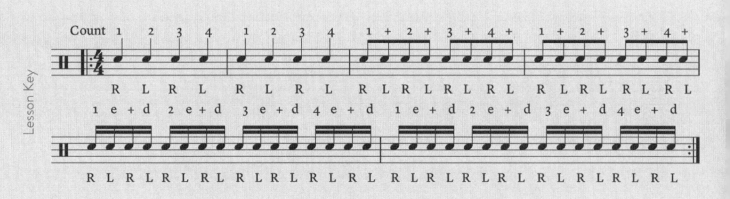

At the start of each rudiment you will see a short two line exercise highlighted in a grey box. I call this The Key. It shows the sticking pattern required to play the rudiment and should be practiced until you feel comfortable at a tempo of around 80 beats per minute. You are now ready to play the subsequent eight rudimental study exercises, which are your building blocks to playing the rudiment around the kit. On the facing page you will see ten exercises developing the rudiment further with suggested drum fill patterns. Once comfortable with these you are encouraged to try your own fills based on the ideas presented.

Drum Kit Notation

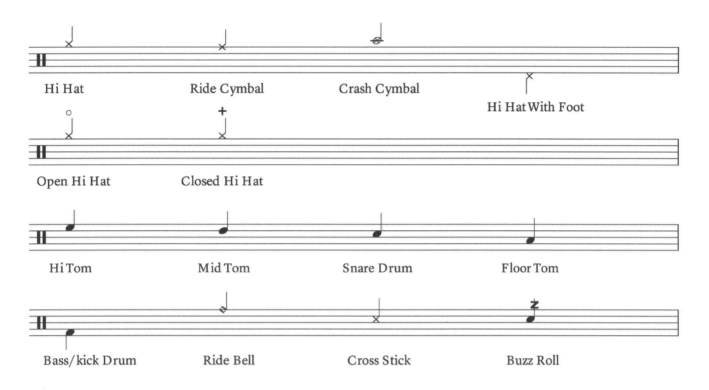

Hi Hat   Ride Cymbal   Crash Cymbal   Hi Hat With Foot

Open Hi Hat   Closed Hi Hat

Hi Tom   Mid Tom   Snare Drum   Floor Tom

Bass/kick Drum   Ride Bell   Cross Stick   Buzz Roll

Drum Roll Example

All the rolls in this book are written as played eg: 9 Stroke Roll

R   R   L   L   R   R   L   L   R

Top tips!

- Learn a new rudiment lesson every one to two weeks.
- Always play to a metronome, starting at a comfortable tempo of around 80 bpm.
- Use The Key as a warm up routine.
- Use these exercises when working towards nationally recognised exams.
- Develop your own grooves and fills based on the ideas in the exercises.
- Find a good local teacher.

Lesson 1
Single Stroke Roll

Lesson 1 (continued)
Single Stroke Roll Around The Kit

Lesson 2
Double Stroke Roll

LESSON 2 **DOUBLE STROKE ROLL**

©BRIAN BESTALL

Lesson 2 (continued)
Double Stroke Roll Around The Kit

Lesson 3
Single Paradiddle

LESSON 3 **SINGLE PARADIDDLE**

©BRIAN BESTALL

Lesson 3 (continued)
Single Paradiddle Around The Kit

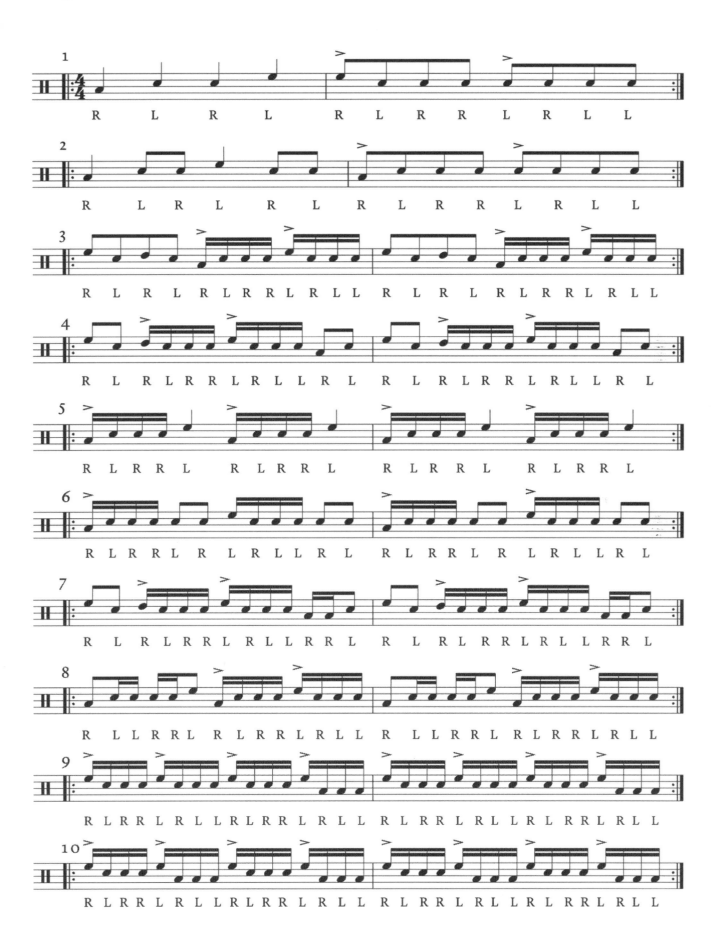

Lesson 4
Flam

Lesson 4 (continued)
Flams Around The Kit

Lesson 5
Drag

LESSON 5 **DRAG** ©BRIAN BESTALL

Lesson 5 (continued)
Drag Played Around The Kit

Lesson 6
Four Stroke Ruff

©BRIAN BESTALL

Lesson 6 (continued)
Four Stroke Ruff Around The Kit

All Ruffs starting with right hand leading

Lesson 7
Five Stroke Roll

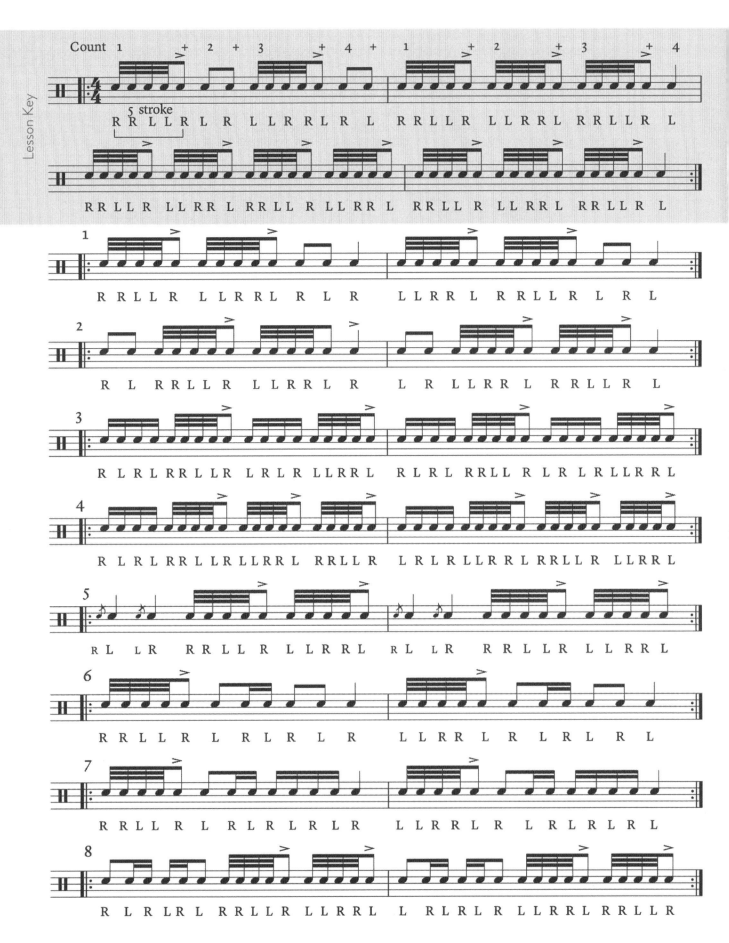

Lesson 7 (continued)
Five Stroke Roll Around The Kit

Lesson 8
Seven Stroke Roll

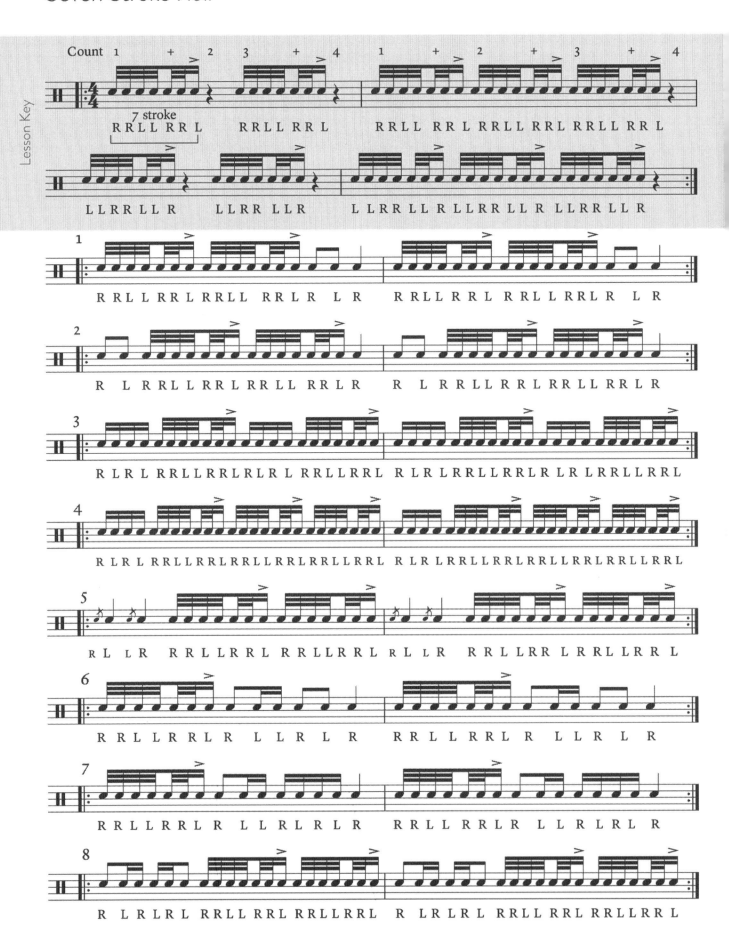

LESSON 8 **SEVEN STROKE ROLL** ©BRIAN BESTALL

Lesson 8 (continued)
Seven Stroke Roll Around The Kit

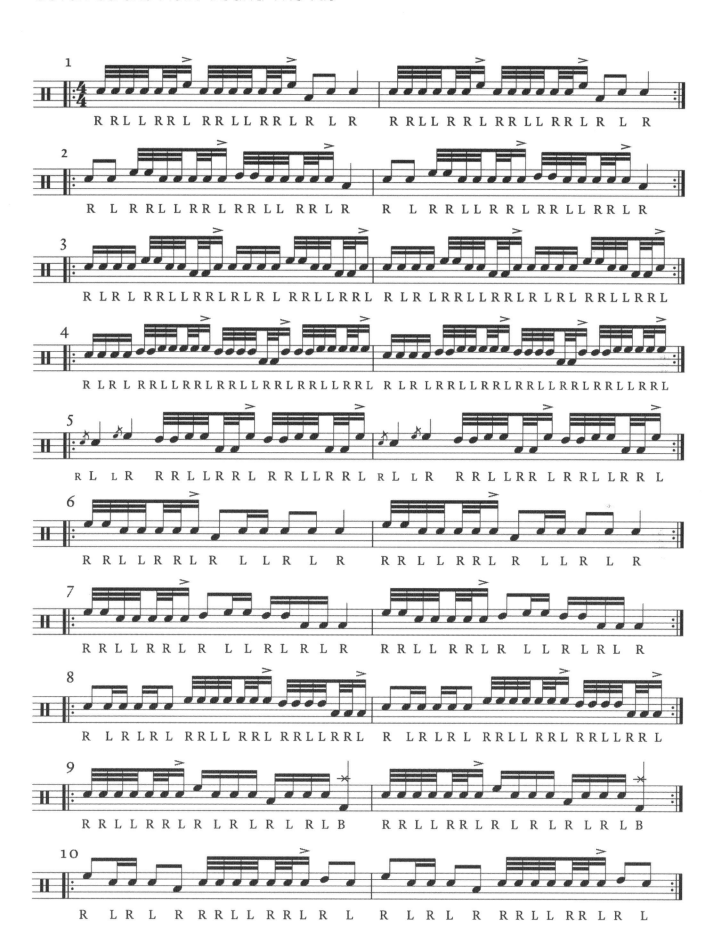

Lesson 9
Nine Stroke Roll

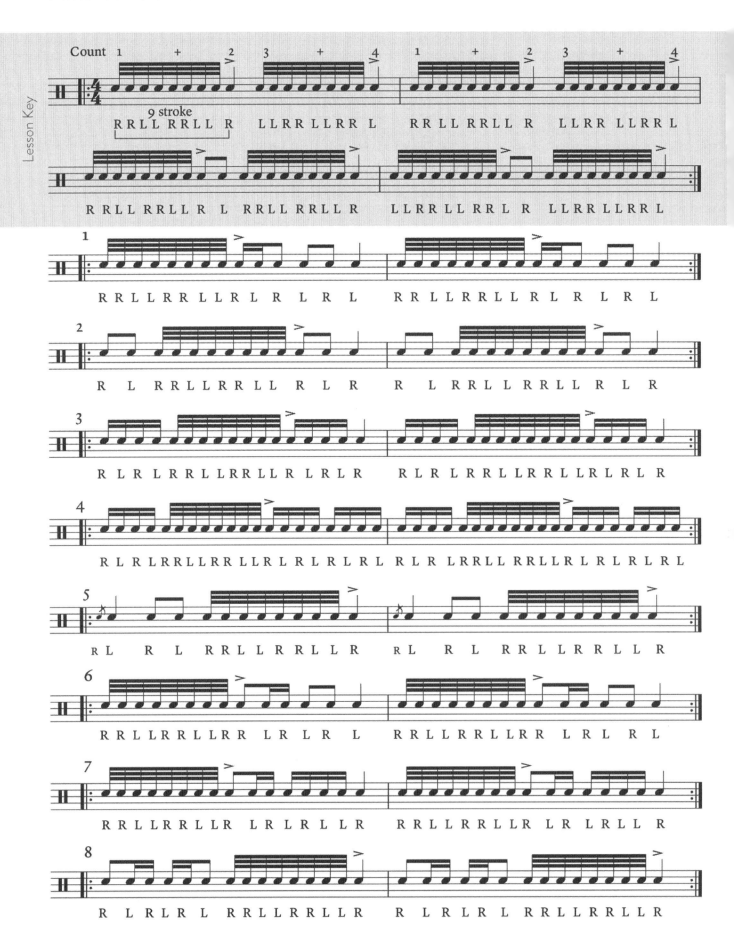

Lesson 9 (continued)
Nine Stroke Roll Around The Kit

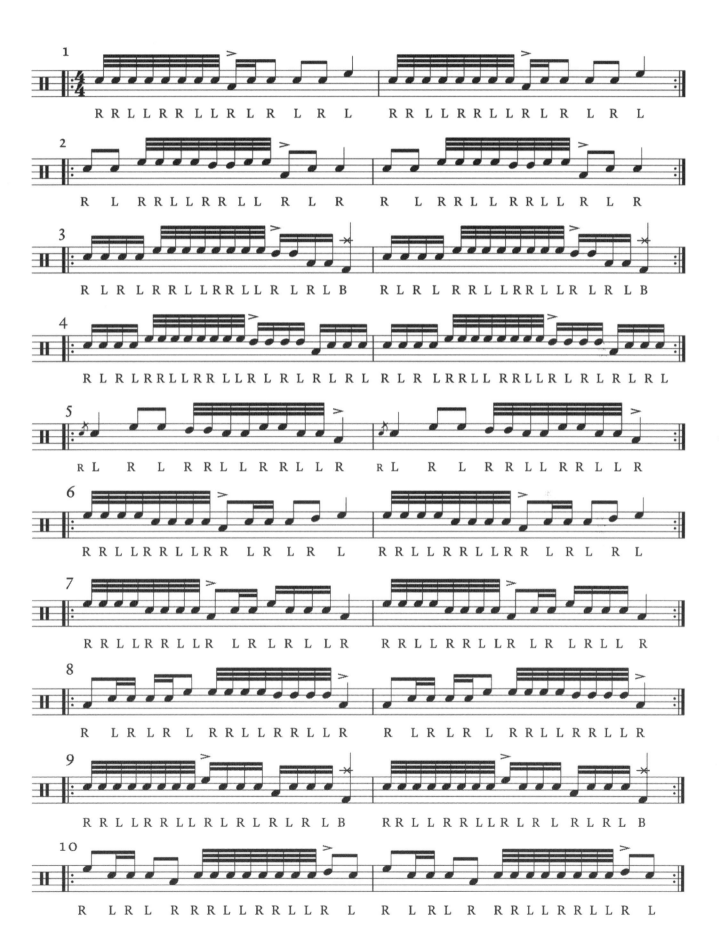

Lesson 10
Flam Tap

©BRIAN BESTALL

Lesson 10 (continued)
Flam Tap Around The Kit

Lesson 11
Flam Accent

Lesson 12
Flamacue

Lesson 12 (continued)
Flamacue Around The Kit

Lesson 13
Flam Paradiddle

LESSON 13 **FLAM PARADIDDLE** ©BRIAN BESTALL

Lesson 13 (continued)
Flam Paradiddle Around The Kit

Lesson 14
Double Paradiddle

Lesson 14 (continued)
Double Paradiddle Around The Kit

Lesson 15
Paradiddle-diddle

LESSON 15 **PARADIDDLE-DIDDLE**

©BRIAN BESTALL

Lesson 15 (continued)
Paradiddle-diddle Around The Kit

Lesson 16
Single Drag and Tap/Stroke (traditional)

Lesson 16 (continued)
Single Drag and Tap/Stroke (traditional) Around The Kit

Lesson 17
Double Drag and Tap/Stroke

LESSON 17 **DOUBLE DRAG AND TAP/STROKE** ©BRIAN BESTALL

Lesson 17 (continued)
Double Drag and Tap/Stroke Around The Kit

Lesson 18
Single Drag Paradiddle or Dragadiddle

Lesson 18 (continued)
Single Drag Paradiddle or Dragadiddle Around The Kit

Lesson 19
Single Ratamacue

LESSON 19 **SINGLE RATAMACUE**

©BRIAN BESTALL

Lesson 19 (continued)
Single Ratamacue Around The Kit

Lesson 20
Double Ratamacue

Lesson 20 (continued)
Double Ratamacue Around The Kit

Lesson 21
Triple Ratamacue

Lesson 21 (continued)
Triple Ratamacue Around The Kit

Lesson 22
Triple Paradiddle

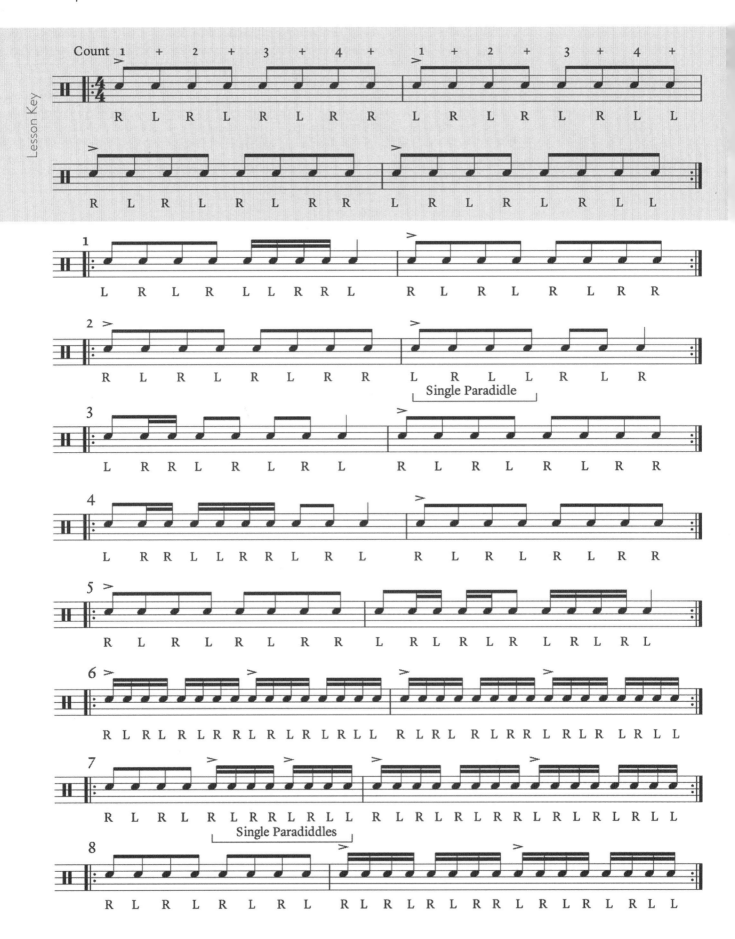

Lesson 22 (continued)
Triple Paradiddle Around The Kit

Lesson 23
Reverse Paradiddle

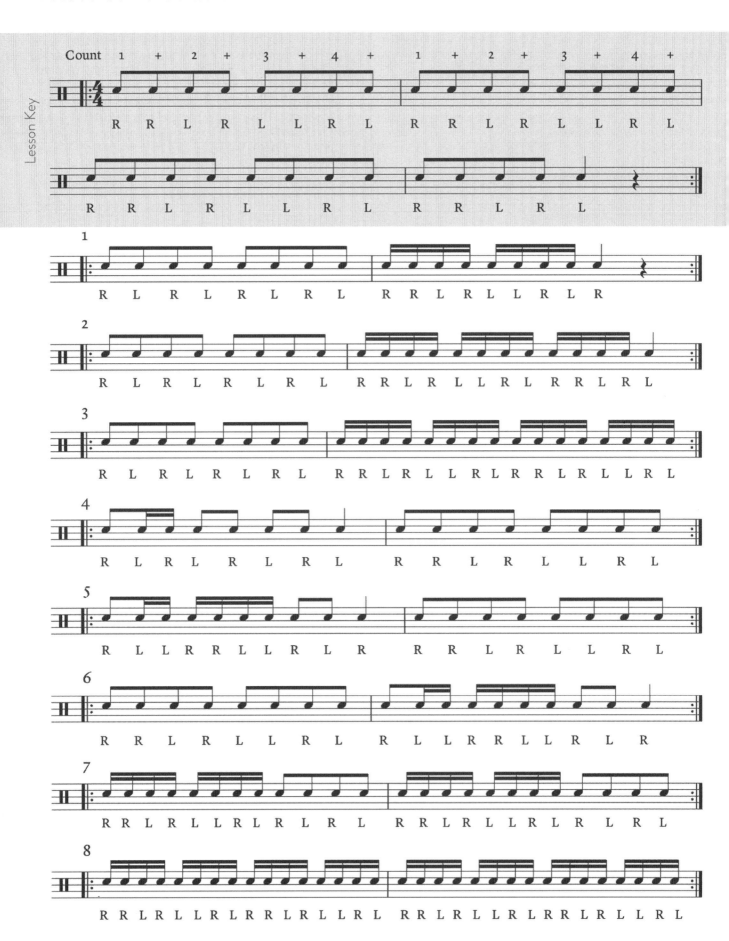

LESSON 23 **REVERSE PARADIDDLE** ©BRIAN BESTALL

Lesson 23 (continued)
Reverse Paradiddle Around The Kit

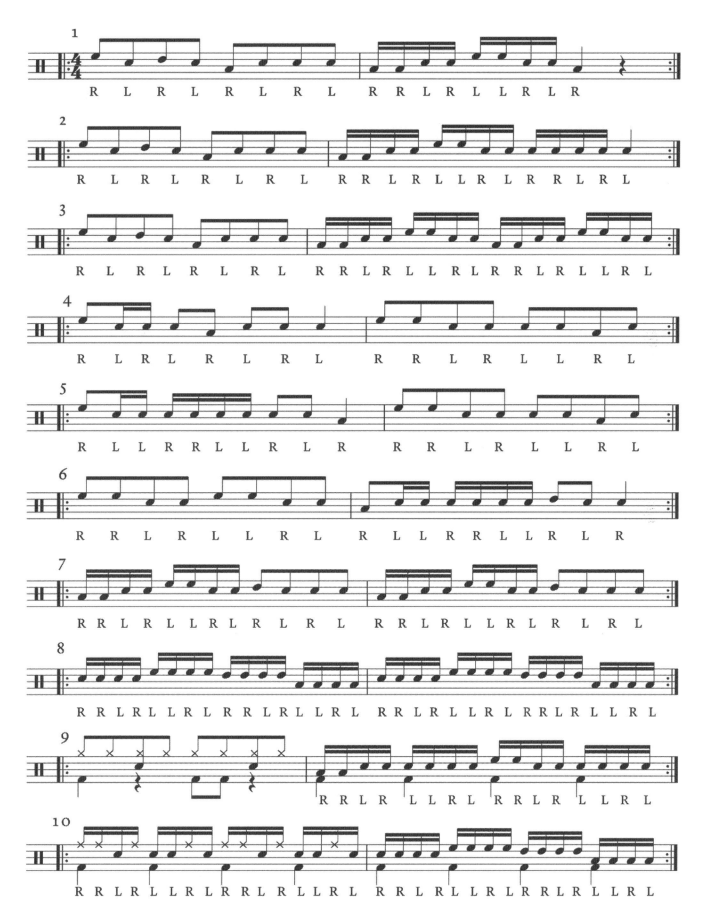

Lesson 24
Pata Fla Fla

Lesson 24 (continued)
Pata Fla Fla Around The Kit

Lesson 25
Swiss Army Triplet

Lesson 25 (continued)
Swiss Army Triplet Around The Kit

Lesson 26
Inward Paraddidle

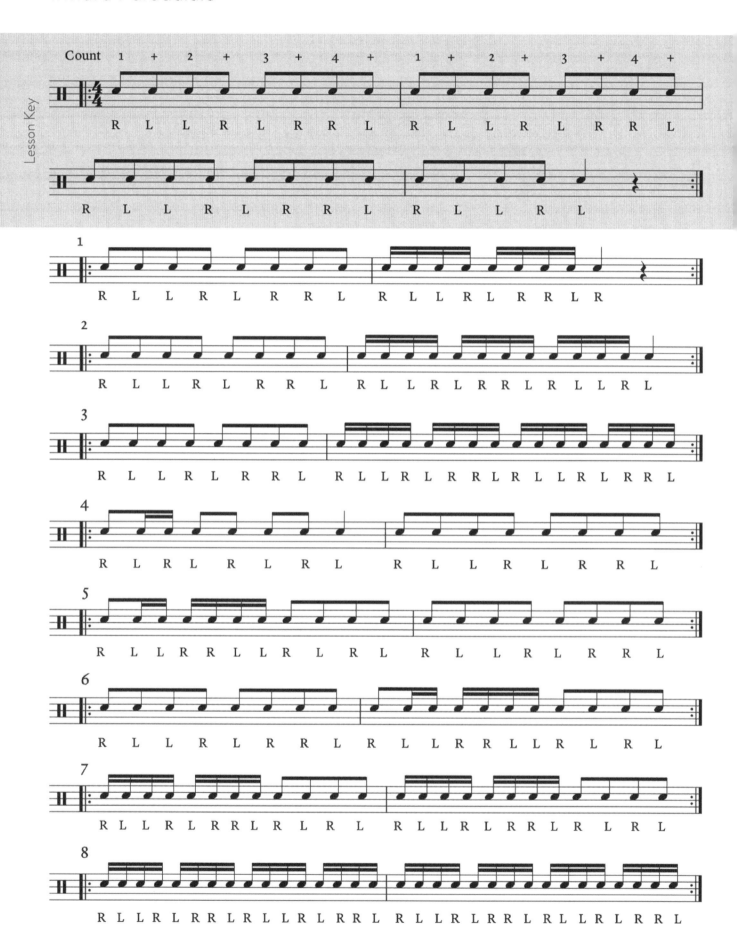

LESSON 26 **INWARD PARADIDDLE**

©BRIAN BESTALL

Lesson 26 (continued)
Inward Paraddidle Around The Kit

Lesson 27
Single Stroke 4

LESSON 27 **SINGLE STROKE 4** ©BRIAN BESTALL

Lesson 28
Multiple Bounce Roll (Buzz Roll)

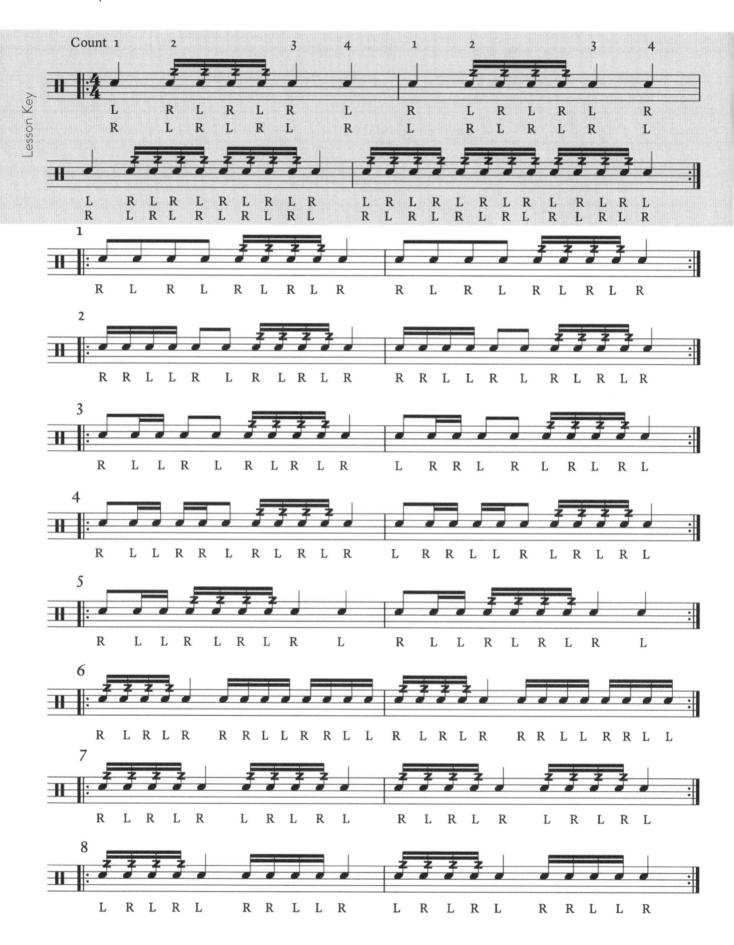

　　　　LESSON 28 **MULTIPLE BOUNCE ROLL (BUZZ ROLL)**　　　　©BRIAN BESTALL

Lesson 28 (continued)
Multiple Bounce Roll (Buzz Roll) Around The Kit

Lesson 29
Triple Stroke Roll

 ©BRIAN BESTALL

Lesson 29 (continued)
Triple Stroke Roll Around The Kit

Lesson 30
Six Stroke Roll

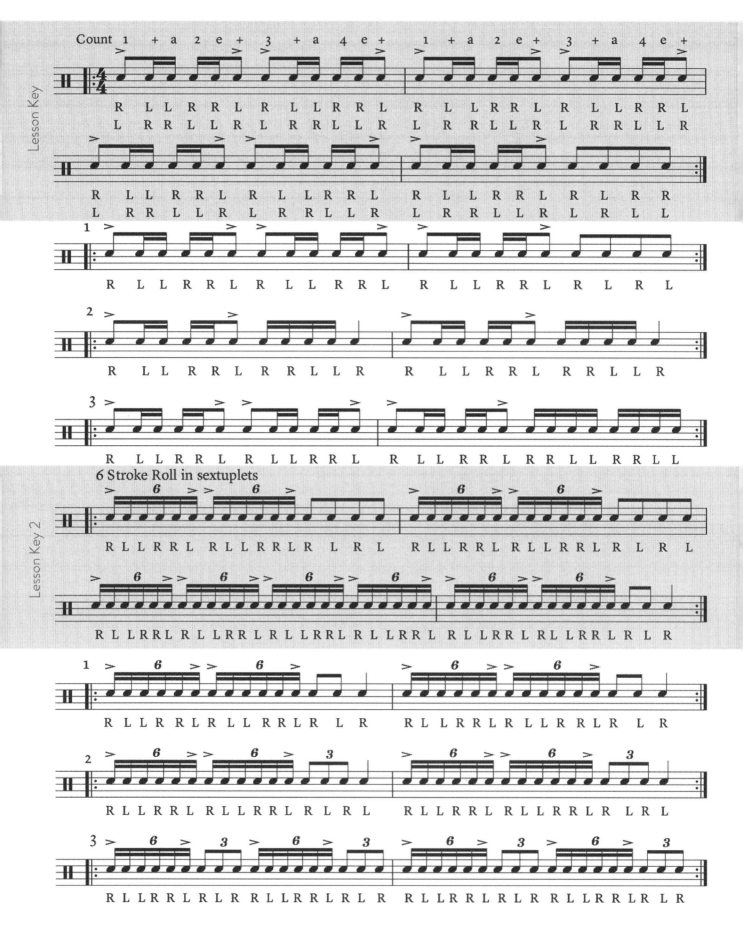

Lesson 30 (continued)
Six Stroke Rol Around The Kit

Lesson 31
Ten Stroke Roll in 4/4 Time

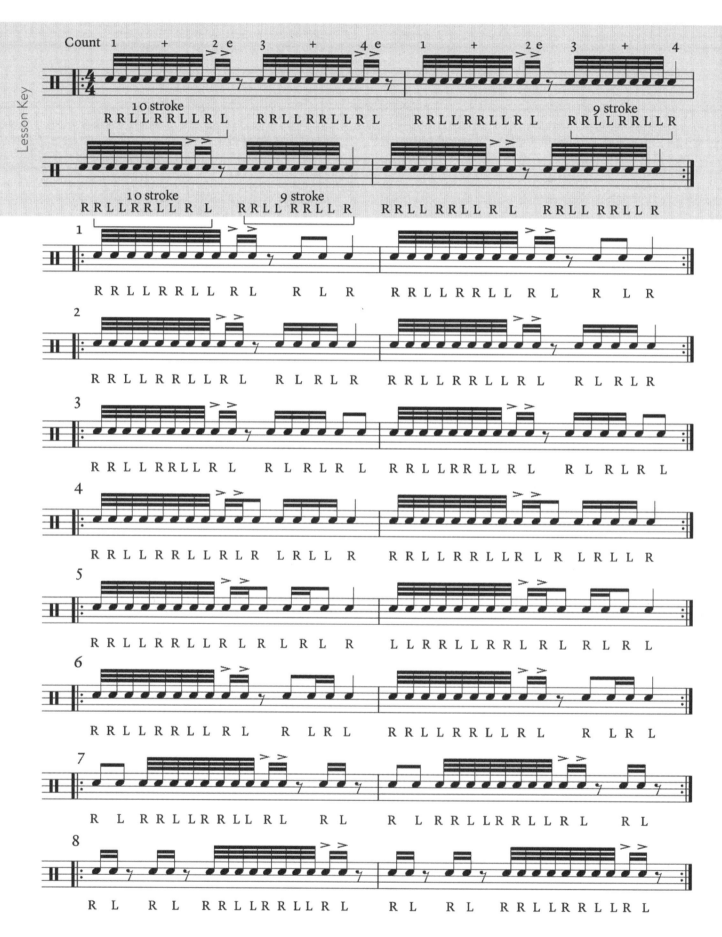

Lesson 31 (continued)
Ten Stroke Roll in 4/4 Time Around The Kit

Lesson 32
Ten Stroke Roll in 3/4 Time, 2 Variations
(variation 1; exercises 1-4, variation 2; exercises 5-8)

LESSON 32 **TEN STROKE ROLL IN 3/4 TIME** ©BRIAN BESTALL

Lesson 32 (continued)
Ten Stroke Roll in 3/4 Time Around The Kit
(exercises 9 & 10 combine both variations)

Lesson 33
Eleven Stroke Roll in 4/4 Time

LESSON 33 **ELEVEN STROKE ROLL IN 4/4 TIME** ©BRIAN BESTALL

Lesson 33 (continued)
Eleven Stroke Roll in 4/4 Time Around The Kit

Lesson 34
Eleven Stroke Roll in 3/4 Time

 ©BRIAN BESTALL

Lesson 34 (continued)
Eleven Stroke Roll in 3/4 Time Around The Kit

Lesson 35
Thirteen Stroke Roll

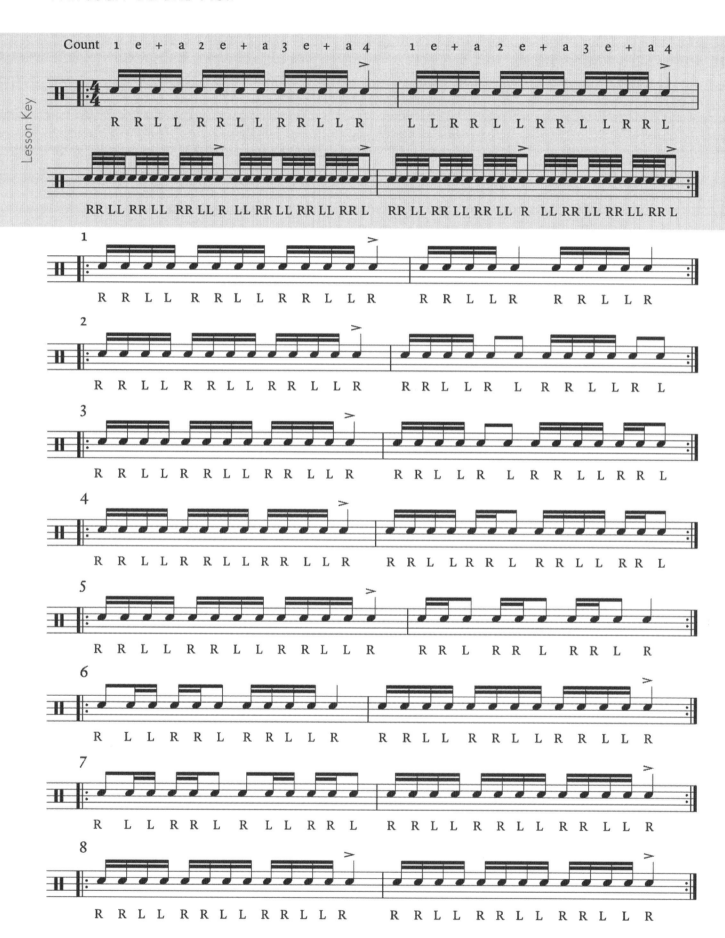

LESSON 35 **THIRTEEN STROKE ROLL** ©BRIAN BESTALL

Lesson 35 (continued)
Thirteen Stroke Roll Around The Kit

Lesson 36
Fifteen Stroke Roll

LESSON 36 **FIFTEEN STROKE ROLL** ©BRIAN BESTALL

Lesson 36 (continued)
Fifteen Stroke Roll Around The Kit

Lesson 37
Seventeen Stroke Roll in 3/4 and 4/4

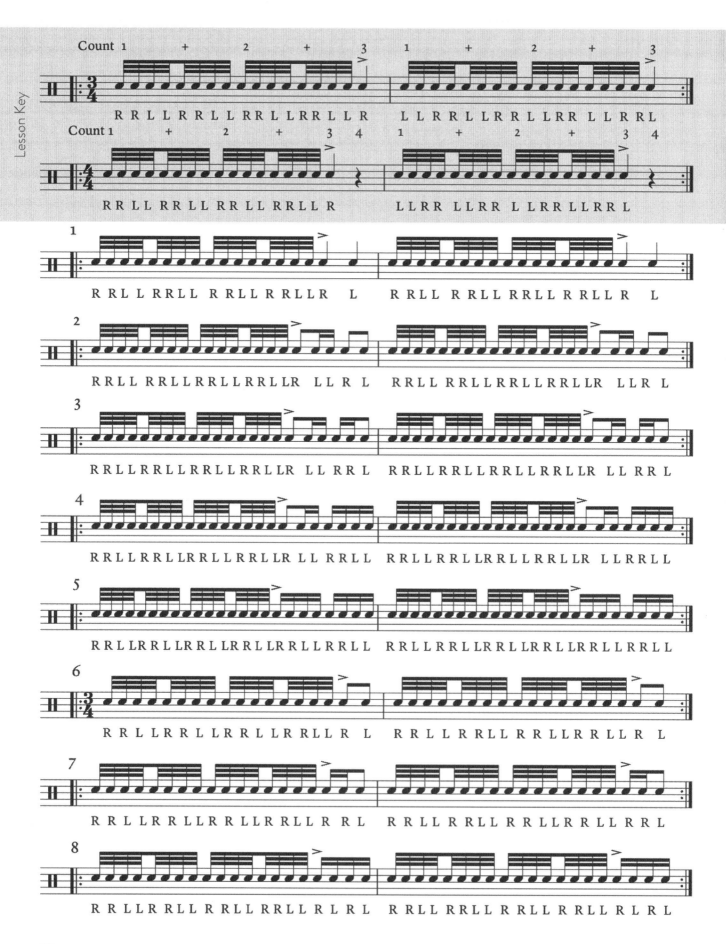

Lesson 37 (continued)
Seventeen Stroke Roll in 3/4 and 4/4 Around The Kit

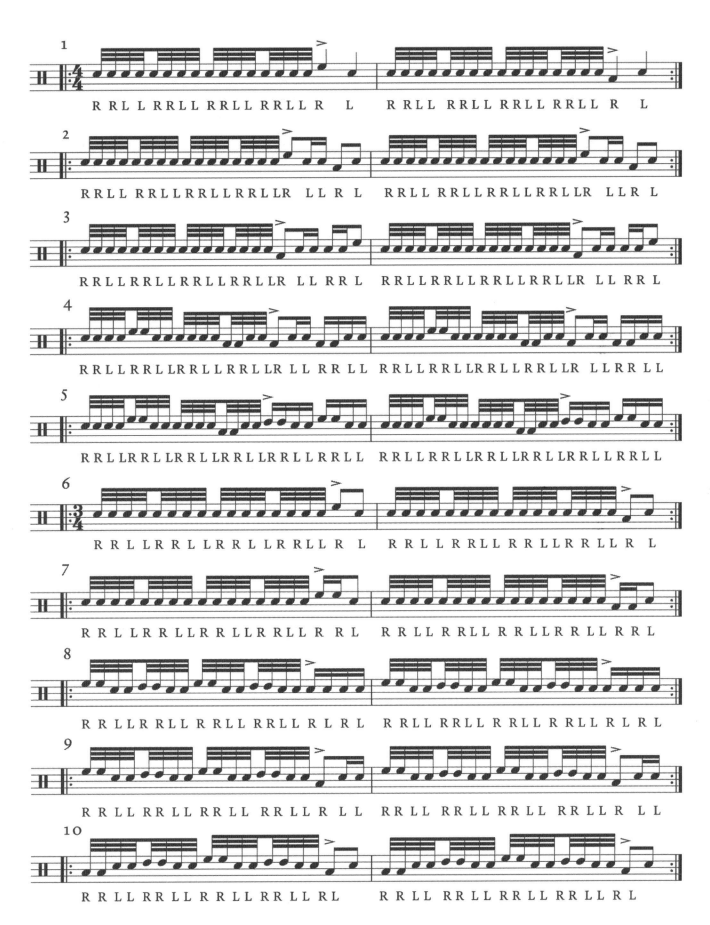

Lesson 38
Flammed Mill

Lesson 39
Flammed Paradiddle-Diddle

Lesson 39 (continued)
Flammed Paradiddle-Diddle Around The Kit

Lesson 40
Inverted Flam Tap

LESSON 40 **INVERTED FLAM TAP** ©BRIAN BESTALL

Lesson 40 (continued)
Inverted Flam Tap Around The Kit

Lesson 41
Flam Drag

Lesson 41 (continued)
Flam Drag Around The Kit

Lesson 42
Lesson 25 (yes it's really called lesson 25)

Lesson 42 (continued)
Lesson 25 Around The Kit

Lesson 43
Drag Paradiddle (number 1)

LESSON 43 **DRAG PARADIDDLE (NUMBER 1)**   ©BRIAN BESTALL

Lesson 43 (continued)
Drag Paradiddle (number 1) Around The Kit

Lesson 44
Drag Paradiddle (number 2)

LESSON 44 **DRAG PARADIDDLE (NUMBER 2)**

©BRIAN BESTALL

Lesson 44 (continued)
Drag Paradiddle (number 2) Around The Kit

Lesson 45
Outward Paradiddle

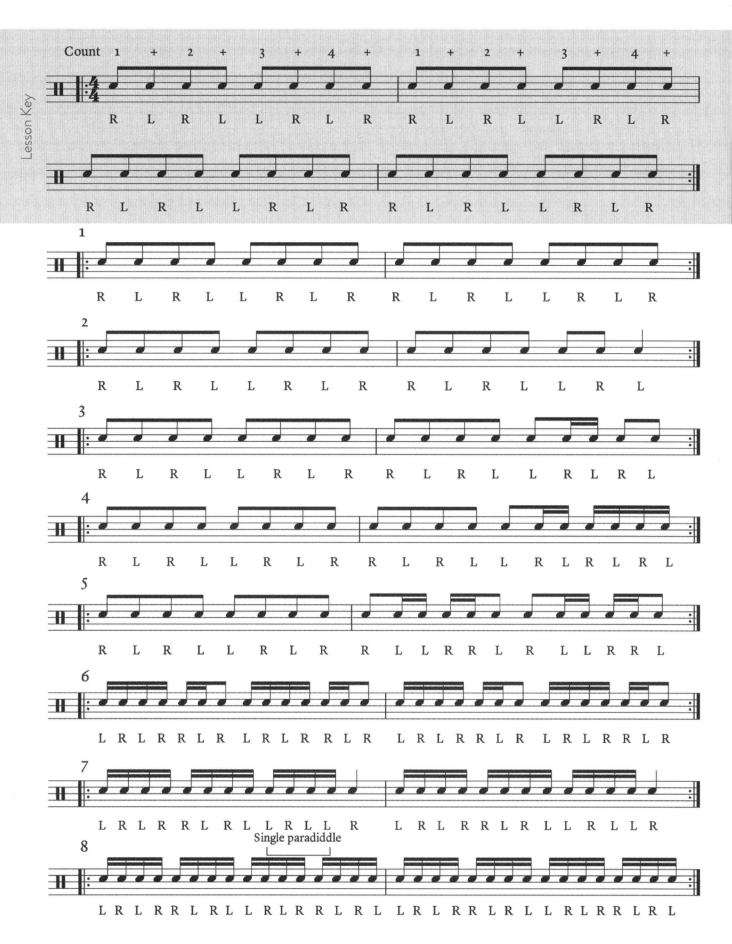

©BRIAN BESTALL

Lesson 45 (continued)
Outward Paradiddle Around The Kit

All The Rudiments At A Glance

All The Rudiments At A Glance (continued)

Use This Page To Log Your Favourite Rudiment Fills

Printed in Great Britain
by Amazon